D1489211

THE
DAILY ZEN
JOURNAL

THE
DAILY ZEN
JOURNAL

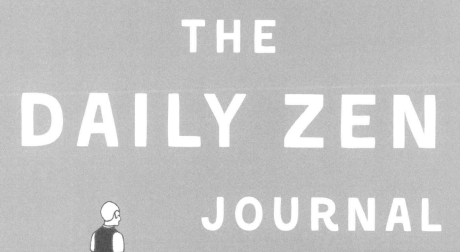

A CREATIVE
COMPANION
FOR A
BEGINNER'S MIND

CHARLIE AMBLER

A TarcherPerigee Book

tarcherperigee

An imprint of Penguin Random House LLC
penguinrandomhouse.com

Illustrations by Iris Gottlieb

TarcherPerigee with tp colophon is a registered trademark of
Penguin Random House LLC.

Most TarcherPerigee books are available at special quantity discounts for bulk
purchase for sales promotions, premiums, fund-raising, and educational needs. Special
books or book excerpts also can be created to fit specific needs. For details, write:
SpecialMarkets@penguinrandomhouse.com.

ISBN 9780143132639

Printed in the United States of America

10 9 8 7 6 5 4 3 2 1

Book design by Pauline Neuwirth

Neither the publisher nor the author is engaged in rendering professional advice or
services to the individual reader. The ideas, procedures, and suggestions contained
in this book are not intended as a substitute for consulting with your physician. All
matters regarding your health require medical supervision. Neither the author nor the
publisher shall be liable or responsible for any loss or damage allegedly arising from any
information or suggestion in this book.

In the beginner's mind, there are many possibilities. In the expert's mind, there are few.

—Zen master Suzuki

WHAT IS BEGINNER'S MIND?

In beginner's mind, we experience the world with fresh eyes, like a child, but with the added consciousness of maturity. Meditation uncovers this essential feeling that is beginner's mind.

WHY SHOULD I CARE?

To embody beginner's mind means to experience life anew, to find joy where you once found boredom and opportunities where you once found obstacles. Beginner's mind isn't the way to happiness—it *is* happiness.

WHERE DO I START?

Right here, right now.

The purpose of this book is not to indoctrinate you with Zen ideology.

It isn't to teach you how to talk the talk, but how to walk the walk:

How to question your thoughts.

How to see every side of things.

How to understand your place in the world—and your place within yourself.

Let thoughts come and go,
but don't serve them tea.

—Zen proverb

Close your eyes for five minutes.

Let your breath flow naturally.

What are the thoughts that come into your mind?

Imagine each thought walking into the room.

Let them come and go on their own.

They are just visitors.

Over time, your experience in meditation comes to resemble "no mind," a pure state in which you can be peaceful and not cling to thoughts.

What does "no mind" mean to you upon first hearing it?

What about beginner's mind?

These exercises are intended to encourage your meditation practice and get you into the zone of beginner's mind.

Practicing every day will help you cultivate a deep mindfulness, a self-awareness, an appreciation of life, and a sense of gratitude toward your loved ones.

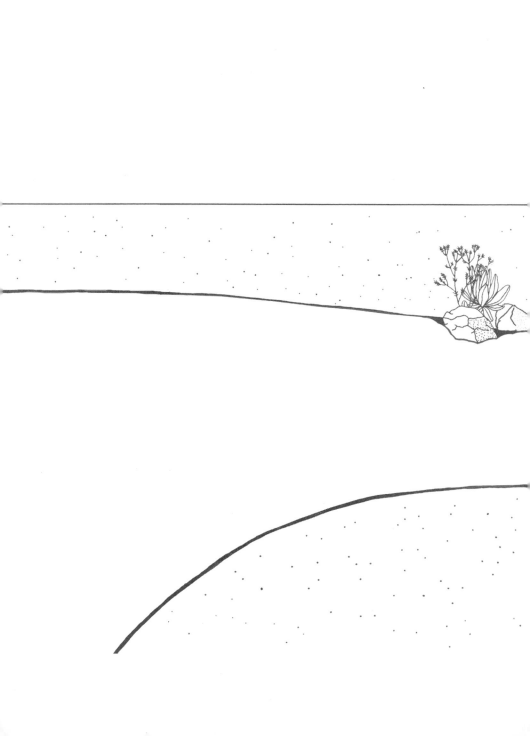

I feel like a kid again when I . . .

Who are you?

Without cultural conditioning?

Without your background?

Without your friends?

Without your job?

Without your stuff?

Who are *you?*

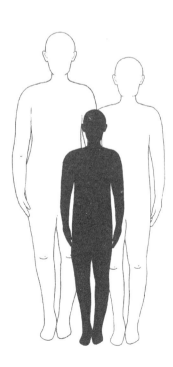

Go outside and stare at the first bit of nature you see. Focus on the details.

What do you see?

Fill the page with observations.

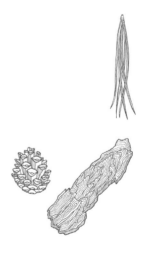

Flowers need dirt to grow, the same way we need suffering, chaos, and difficulty in order to learn patience, joy, and peace.

The way up a mountain is never a straight line, and the journey can be different for everyone.

Nature helps us get out of our heads and see the world as it is. We can understand it better through metaphor. Make up some of your own natural metaphors below:

Set a timer for ten minutes.

Sit comfortably in a chair, but don't rest your head, so you don't fall asleep!

Let's meditate.

Breathe in, 1.
Out, 2.
In, 3.
Out, 4.
Go to 10.
Return to 1.

If you lose count, return to 1.

Don't force the breath—just let it flow naturally.

Thoughts will come and go.

Distractions will try to grab at you.

If you lose count (you will), go back to 1.

Eventually you won't need to count. But for now, try to practice this at least once a day. Try to add five minutes to your practice each week.

Practicing for twenty to thirty minutes a day is a solid foundation for mindfulness.

What popped into your head during this first sitting?

What is "just sitting"?

It's the meditative state in which your thoughts have faded away and you can simply be. Each day, we practice meditation. Some days we can "just sit." But when we strive for this, it's much harder.

Over time, this meditative consciousness trains your brain to stop clinging so much in daily life. You can be at peace with "just being," the same way you find peace in "just sitting."

This is beginner's mind. There are no burdens—you are at play and at peace.

How would you behave if you had no competitors?

No ambitions?

What would you do?

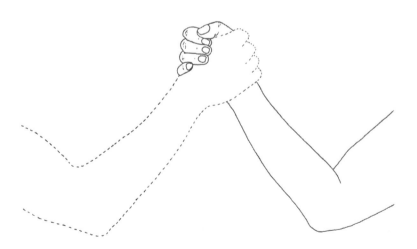

What would make your life lighter
if you removed it?

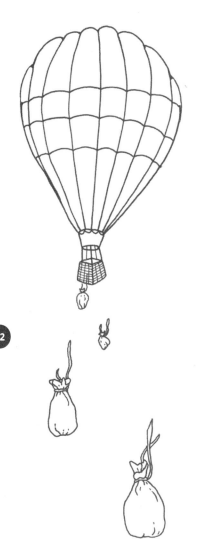

What you're holding on to in the past:

What you're planning for the future:

What does it feel like to spin around in this cycle?

23

What would letting go mean to you?

Okay, now meditate again for ten minutes.

Afterward, fill the bubbles with the thoughts that emerge.
Don't force them. They'll come on their own.

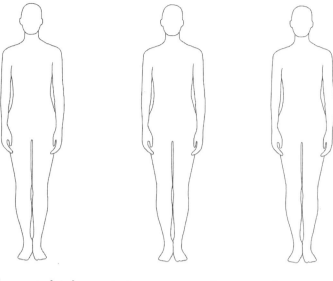

Who you think
you are:

Who you try to be:

Who you are:

The true self is who you are beneath all your layers of assumptions, ideas, and conditioning. Listen to your true self. Take some time if you have to.

What are you trying to tell yourself?

What is it like to be you?

The wise adapt themselves to circumstances, as water molds itself to the pitcher.

—Zen proverb

In what ways have you changed shape throughout your life?

BREATHE

Take a photo of this page and set it as your phone wallpaper.

What are some of your oldest habits?

How can you make them new again?

Pretend you're a beginner at your activities for a week, from hobbies to chores.

What new experiences and
insights emerged?

What does your mind do when you let go of all thoughts?
What does it produce without effort?

In Zen and Taoism, *wu wei*, or action through nonaction,
is important. We often do too much, creating chaos where
simplicity would otherwise reign.

When we step back and let nature work with us, we have
the assistance of a very powerful friend.

When you imagine the ideal simple life, what are its core features? What does it feel like?

List of things you believe right now:

List of things you believed five years ago:

Each week, see if you can increase your practice by five minutes. Slow and steady wins the race—except there is no race.

You should meditate for twenty
minutes a day unless you're too busy.
Then you should meditate for an hour.

—Zen proverb

INFORMATION: Consumed

Examples:

KNOWLEDGE: Experienced

Examples:

WISDOM: Uncovered

Examples:

Throughout this life, you can never be certain of living long enough to take another breath.

—Huang Po

Close your eyes.

Imagine a horror movie about your life. The bad guy is after everything you love.

Write what those things are on this movie poster.

Plot your future year by year.

Now tear this page out and rip it up.

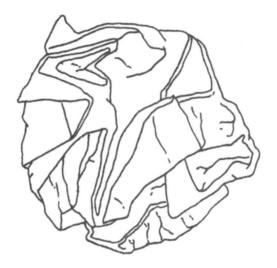

To be present doesn't mean to be reckless, but to appreciate each day fully. Instead of planning too far ahead, be grateful!

WRITE A LETTER CATCHING UP WITH YOURSELF.

Store it away. Dig it up in a year.

46

With some email providers, you can choose to send yourself an email reminder in a year. This is a good way to do this exercise.

Things you believe but are afraid to share with others:

The foolish reject what they see.

The wise reject what they think.

—Zen proverb

When have you rejected what you saw?

What happened?

Write down everything you're afraid to let go.

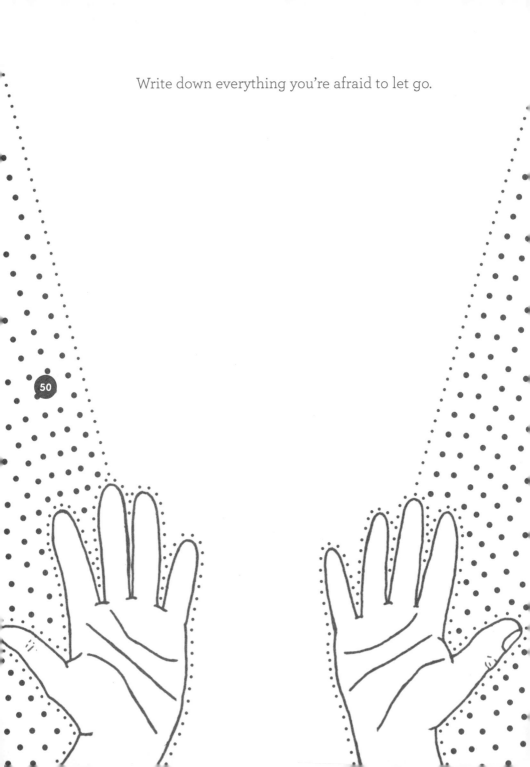

Write down everything you have but don't care about.

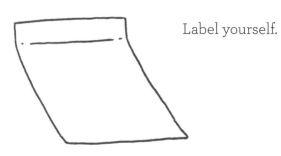

Label yourself.

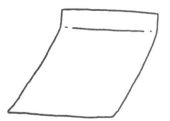

How do these labels comfort you?

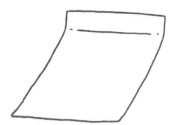

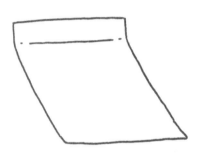

How do they limit you?

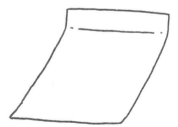

In meditation, you will experience brief moments of thoughtless bliss.

They come when you least expect them.

This is called *samadhi,* or stillness of mind.

What feelings emerge from this consciousness?

A problem you're trying to solve:

Write down the simplest, dumbest questions you can think of relating to it.

Answer them slowly and methodically, building up from there.

The answers to complex problems are often very simple, and yet we overlook them, thinking we need complex solutions.

This time take something bothering you and break it down into its smallest atoms:

A tree in the wind.

The wind in a tree.

All in me.

—Zen koan

READ THE SILENCE.

What does it mean to be aware?

What does it mean to be compassionate?

What does it mean to be honest?

Who is your nemesis?

Write that person a love letter.

We obsess over money and work and yet waste much of our attention on meaningless distractions.

Fill out this pie chart to reflect how you use your attention.

How do you want to use your attention?

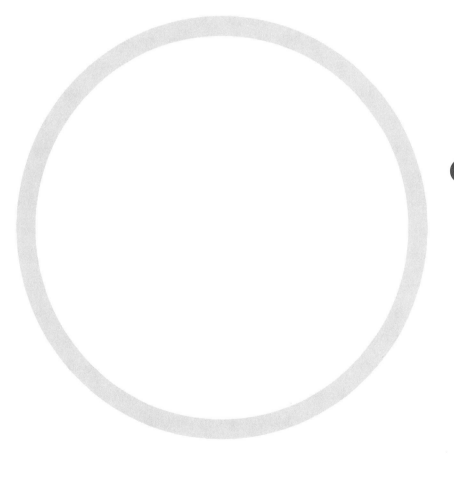

DON'T TRY . . .

DO TRY

Two men were arguing about a flag flapping in the wind. "It's the wind that is really moving," stated the first one.

"No, it is the flag that is moving," contended the second. A Zen master, who happened to be walking by, overheard the debate and interrupted them.

"Neither the flag nor the wind is moving," he said. "It is the mind that moves."

You are a stone thrown into a pond.

Write along the ripples how you abstractly have an impact on other people.

Imagine the weird far-reaching impacts of your tiny actions.

See how far you can go.

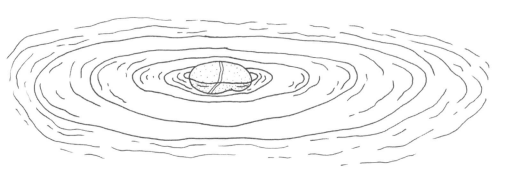

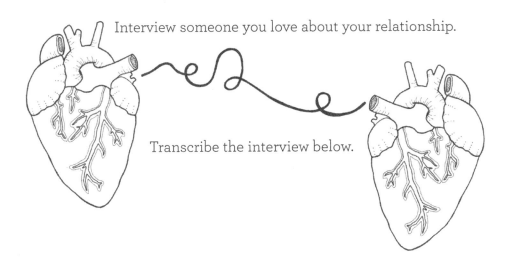

Interview someone you love about your relationship.

Transcribe the interview below.

Interview a stranger about something he or she cares about.

Transcribe the interview below.

Before enlightenment—chop wood, carry water. After enlightenment— chop wood, carry water.

—Zen proverb

Enlightenment is nothing special. It's just when you experience a pure awareness of the present moment.

Meditation helps us bring these moments of enlightenment into consciousness more often.

What were your recent moments of enlightenment?

What makes you glad to be alive?

Make a list of everything you're grateful for. Save it someplace where you'll see it regularly. I took a photo of mine and emailed it to myself.

Try doing a walking meditation.

Let go of a different thought or attachment with each step.

With beginner's mind, every activity can be a type of meditation. What do you do that you could use as an exercise in mindfulness? For me, running, playing drums, and writing are all opportunities to meditate.

Think of an opinion you strongly disagree with.

Write a letter arguing in favor of it.

Be like water.

Picture yourself as:

> An ocean.
> A pond.
> A stream.
> A puddle.
> A raindrop.
> A cloud.
> In a glass.
> In a tub.
> In a pool.

Be flexible and transparent.

Let yourself adapt to every situation and experience.

Flexibility and fluidity make us strong;
rigidity and stubbornness
often hold us back.

Sometimes our opinions prevent us from understanding other people. Attempt to see through the eyes of your adversaries. This helps build compassion for all beings, hard as it may be!

**If you understand,
things are just as they are.**

**If you do not understand,
things are just as they are.**

—Zen proverb

Fill the page with questions to yourself.

Close your eyes. Imagine the world as yourself.

What comes to mind?

Now imagine yourself as the world.

What does this conjure up?

Things I can control:

Things I can't control:

83

How is your life like a work of art?

How could you act more like its creator?

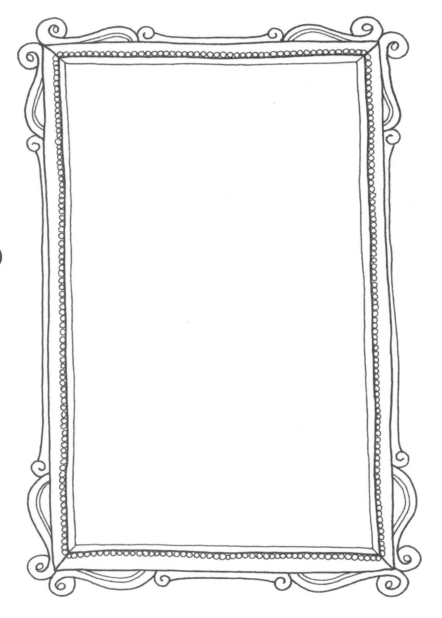

Suffering can be good for you.

There's no strength without resistance,
no night without day.

Reflect on a time when your pain has made
you stronger. How? Why?

Congratulations, you've just won the lottery.
Money is no longer a concern.

Theoretically, how would you spend your time?

Write things you're afraid of on the mirror.

Find a mirror in your house and tell yourself why you're afraid of these things.

Make eye contact!

Fill the page up with your most precious opinions.

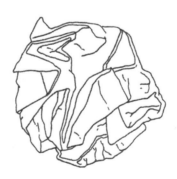

Rip out the page, crumple it up, and play trash-can basketball.

What do you dislike most in other people?

What are your pet peeves?

For each one, explain why.

List a big goal.

Break it up into ten smaller goals.

Break up each of these ten goals into three smaller ones.

Go as far as you can.

Write ten complaints.

1.

2.

3.

4.

5.

6.

7.

8.

9.

10.

Reframe them as jokes.

1.

2.

3.

4.

5.

6.

7.

8.

9.

10.

What are your worst habits? What do you consider your vices? What kinds of trouble have they caused you?

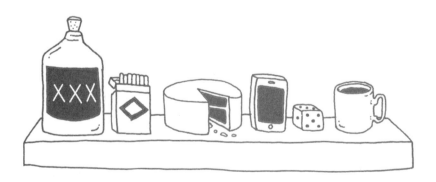

What's your morning routine?

Tomorrow, perform it backwards.

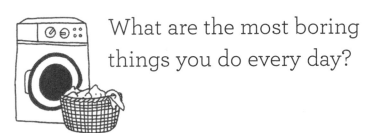

What are the most boring things you do every day?

Tomorrow, make a point of treating
each boring task as a meditation.

How did you feel after doing this?

In what ways do you perform in your daily life?

What activities are you obligated to do even
if they don't feel natural?

The reverse side

also has a reverse side.

—Zen proverb

The reverse side
also has a reverse side.

—Zen proverb

List ten people you love.

How would your relationships with them change if you were perfectly honest with them at all times?

With each in-breath, inhale a worry.

With each out-breath, let it go.

The obstacle is the path.

—Zen proverb

NOTHING IS PERMANENT

Tear this page out and tack it somewhere
you look every day.

The reward of patience is patience.

—Saint Augustine

What do you do that is completely unnecessary?

What do you do that is utterly essential?

Things you know only from books:

Things you know only from experience:

How have you changed
over the past . . .

one year?

five years?

ten years?

one week?

one month?

one day?

We like to pretend we're set in stone, but we're always changing. Beginner's mind is recognizing this perpetual state of flux.

What is most important to you in life?

Why?

Why?

Why?

Why?

Why?

WHAT'S HOLDING YOU BACK?

WHAT IS CURRENTLY WORRYING YOU?

Imagine what the worst outcome is
for each concern.

If you can make peace with a worst-case scenario, you will
remain calm regardless of the outcome.

A windmill's true power is
revealed only when it faces the wind;
a person's, only when he
faces adversity.

—Zen proverb

Close your eyes. Listen to the voice in your head.

What is it telling you?

Label each with your attachments.

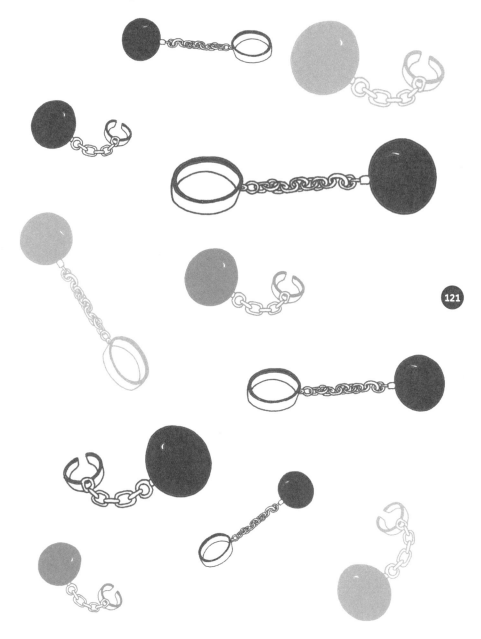

Do something you suck at every day.

What will you do today?

We spend so much time doing, striving, wanting, thinking, but meditation is a process of undoing. It's a counterbalance to all the drama we create in our lives.

 What do you *need* to undo?

 What do you *want* to undo?

What things would be better if simplified?

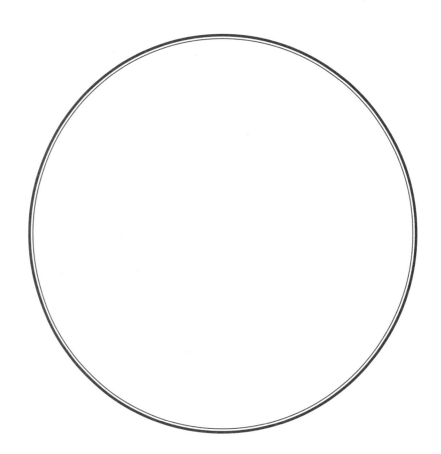

What are your happiest and most vivid memories
from childhood?

They all contain the essence of beginner's mind.
How can you cultivate this for yourself now?

What are some dark memories from your past?
What's your baggage?

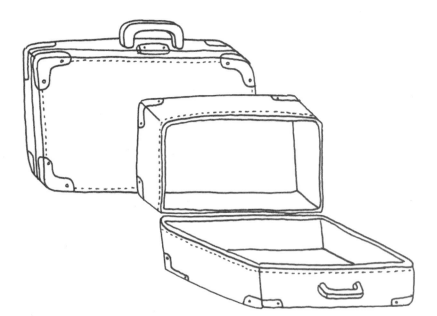

The next time you meditate, don't keep the darkness out. Let it enter the room and sit with you. See what it says, what it teaches you. In Zen, we acknowledge both light and darkness as teachers.

The darkness says:

If today happened to be the last day of your life, what would you do? This seems like a corny idea, but have you actually tried it? It's quite powerful.

Fill this page with questions
to yourself.

Things that are true:

Things that I wish were true:

Let go or be dragged.

—Zen proverb

Write down your deepest secrets.

Cool, thanks. Now they're not secrets.

Think of your most recent confrontation.

What you wanted to happen:

What actually happened:

How you reacted:

What you'd do differently next time:

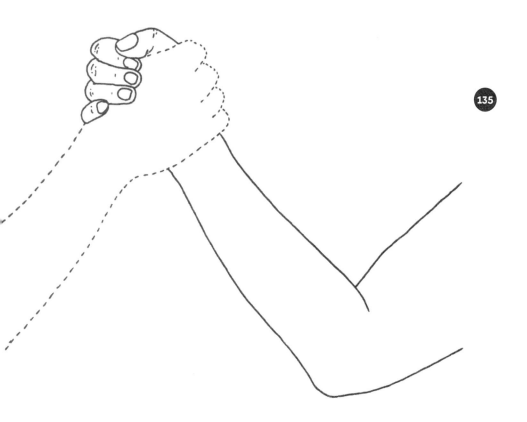

Draw the circle as slowly and mindfully as you possibly can. Keep your breathing steady.

This is active meditation.

See how smoothly you can draw it.

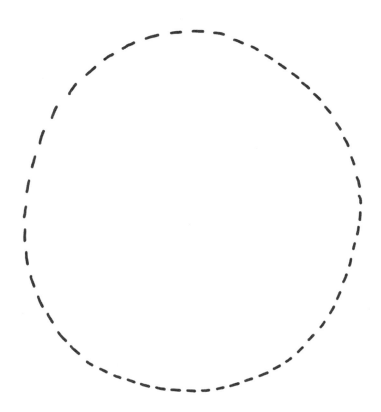

Write three tiny thank-you notes to special people in your life. Cut them out and send them.

How can I be kind today?

How can I be genuine today?

How can I be peaceful today?

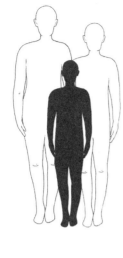

Your ego holds you back.

Your true self sets you free.

What defines your ego?

What defines your true self?

Be wherever you are.

Where are you?

How are you? Dig deep.

Why do you so earnestly seek
the truth in distant places?
Look for delusion and truth in the
bottom of your own heart.

—Ryokan

What I crave

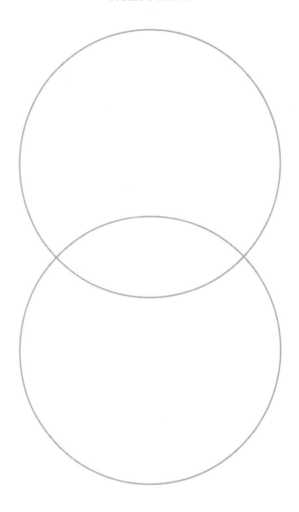

What I avoid

Fill the page with as many tiny circles as you can possibly fit here. Try to savor the creation of each one, no matter how small or inconsequential it seems.

When we treat small tasks with the utmost care, the meaning of life becomes clearer. Momentary mindfulness brings peace and balance.

Now draw the void.

Do not follow the ideas of others, but learn to listen to the voice within yourself.

—Zen proverb

What does the voice within you say right now?

What is your biggest task or problem right now?

Write five different ways of approaching it.

How can you see it anew?

Let the mind be like the lake that reflects all of the clouds passing over it without any sticking to it.

—Zen proverb

Over the next twenty-four hours, see if you can meditate whenever you have a free moment. Even if it's just for a few seconds.

Observations:

When was the last time you were totally wrong about something or someone? Describe it in detail.

Nothing is as it seems,
nor is it otherwise.

—Zen proverb

Okay, our journey together is almost done. After all these exercises, what does "no mind" mean to you?

What does "beginner's mind" mean to you now?

This week, do something you suck at for at least an hour.

What was it?

How did it feel?

By avoiding things we're bad at, we avoid failure. When we avoid failure, we avoid risk. When we avoid risk, we avoid life and severely limit ourselves.

How do you limit yourself in this way?

157

Forgiveness is a type of beginner's mind. We're returning to a fresh place without baggage or spite.

What do you need to let go of in order to forgive others?

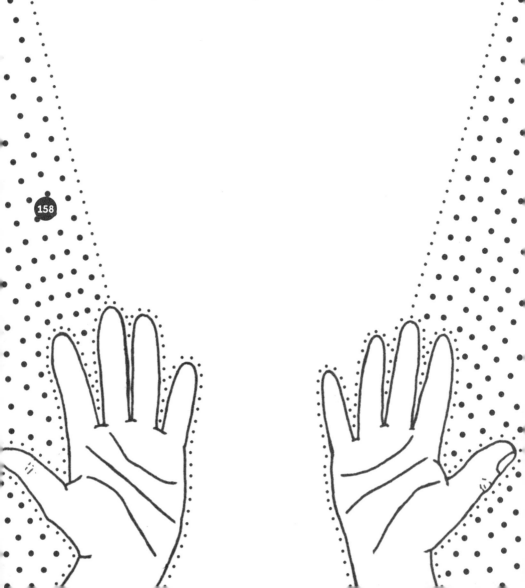

How have you wronged others? If you asked for forgiveness, what would it mean to them?

Sometimes life sucks.

This passes.

Sometimes life is great.

This passes too.

How would you act differently if you were totally yourself at all times?

Theoretically, if you found out that everything you know is wrong, how would you react? What would you do?

What could you do to encourage others to be more open and honest with you?

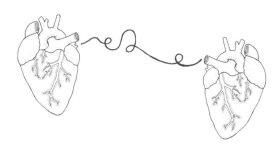

Weekly Checklist

☐ Daily meditation

☐ A good book

☐ A quality conversation

☐ Gratitude

☐ Small act of kindness

☐ Small act of simplification

☐ Self-care

☐ Time with nature or animals

☐ Time with loved ones

☐ Time with yourself

Before we go, give yourself some space.

MEDITATION NOTES

MEDITATION NOTES

MEDITATION NOTES

MEDITATION NOTES

MEDITATION NOTES

MEDITATION NOTES